May all the lines you make through life.

Walburg

forgetting forgi

'There is an ancient tradition of sending Walburga cards o.
80's when I forgot to send a girlfriend a Valentine. Instead
book and picked Walburga as Patron Saint of the forgetfu
turned out she was an Anglo-Saxon and sister of St Willibald and St Winnibald. She and her brothers helped convert the Germans to Christianity. She later became Abbess of one of the most important monasteries in central Europe: but, unlike Hildergard of Bingen, she never wrote tunes or descriptions of her libido, so modern fashion has passed her by.'

Bradwan Nationwide Cultural Guide to Preston, City Gent, Issue 98.

Most of this book comes from pen drawn and photocopied Walburga and Christmas 'cards' made between 1982 and 1998. The constraints of photocopying meant they were in the style of wood engravings. I made a very few of a tiny, hand made, collection in 1996. Then in 2002-04, when I was struck down by pneumonia and unable to work, I used a Mac and a scanner to create a hand made 'beta' version of this book; which I printed, folded, trimmed, sewed, and glued myself.

My maternal grandfather was technically illiterate, yet ran a farm, a timber business, and made wheels and coffins for his village in Finnish Karelia. I remembered him when I set out to manufacture the book. Teaching myself bookbinding seemed like small fish compared to putting an iron tyre on a wooden wheel. Forming the company to publish this book was more complex, but no more so than calculating volumes and prices of cut timber without knowing how to write formal numbers.

This 'externally' printed edition has the same poems and pictures as the 'hand-made' one, although re-scanned, and with eight additional pages.

I was born in Gorseinon; grew up in Crawley, where I went to Thomas Bennett Comprehensive; and have spent most of my life in Bradford. I will probably still have a Bradford City season ticket when you read this, if they still exist.

My biggest literary influence is J.L. Carr, whose example prompted my writing, drawing and publishing. I also value J.B. Priestley's work. My poetry owes much to John Lillison and Rodney Spelvin: although I now belong wholeheartedly to the school of Alaric Gilpin.

A lot of my imagery comes from the iconography of St Walburga, details of which can be found in:
'The Book of Saints, Dom. Basil Watkins (Ed), A&C Black, 2002.'

Glyn Watkins 9th May, 25th August 2003, 29th March and 26th March 2004

Wind wafts gently
    on fields of grain
Rippling the surface
    of fancy's fruiting
Growth from where
    no shields have lain
Drawing from life
    love's deep rooting

As you sail
Through seas of pain
And piracy of hate
your life is looting
Drawing on your depths
don't fain
Let the oil of love
be the well that's shooting

Come, come, return Sun of man

Kindling of hope brought from afar

Beacon of light stored in the soul

Spirit be true, or bought in a can

But faith no darkness can mar

So let joy be the peal of the welcomers toll

— Whyjon Boathocks —

Broadcasting seeds
casting grains to fate
with hope of sun
of rain
on harvests await
what's scythed then feeds

passion broadcast
lasting death negates
let joy's oil run
soothing pain
lets conquer hate
just love will last

Five

The space of infinity may
    wrap us all
But the motes that are hope
Show we don't stand
    in a cold empty hall
The light that is feeding
Show it's not vain to call
Above the noise of the speeding
And the grief of a pall
To the sound that is leading
To the love for us all
None walk alone
If with love
You stand tall

Seven

Cold, Cold as the clay
But it doesn't die or fade
Still, waits to see the day
When it's promises are paid.

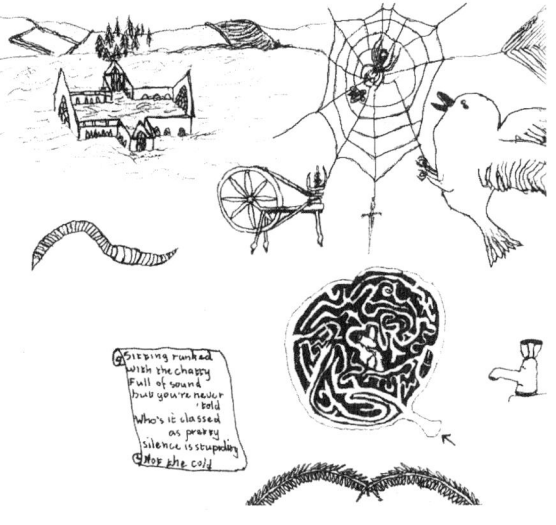

Undeclared interest

The soft edge
of your beauty
wont stand against
the hard edge of the duty
your blinding truths demand.

You can hear the ones that guide us
to burning of despair
but believe this fool that will cuss
the fool that does declare.

Truth don't stand with reason
your mirror does nought but blind
you see a deserved lesion
I see your beauty underlined.

Poetic sparks of a stranger
wont pay your penitents fee
but warm them in hopes manger
and the worth of living
      you'll see.

Fields of Dreams

The boundaries broken
The peeling of walls
Destruction's grim token
Destruction appals

The press that's marking
The face of the carer
The mouths that are barking
At knowledge's barer

The voice's demanding
The calls on the time
The pleasures remanding
The passing of prime.
BUT
There are motes in the darkening
Catching the shaft of the truth
The light that is harkening
The life that is youth.

The future's strong trees
Begun with a seed
Of knowledge that frees
From fear and from greed
The turning the clay
The tilling and sowing
The work and the play
The life and the growing
SO
Don't let the soul cower
Live joyous schemes
And see the love flower
In more fields of dreams

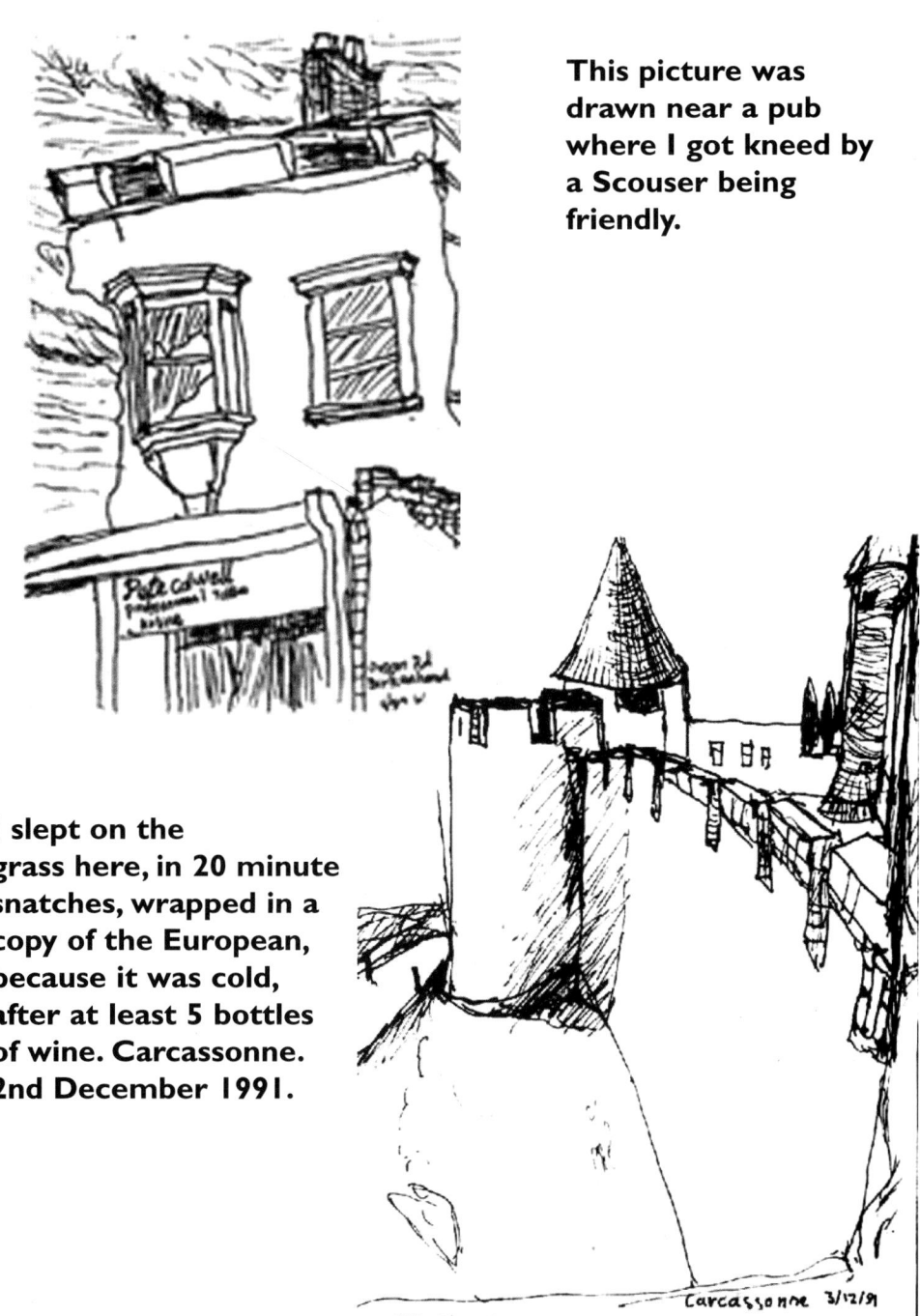

This picture was drawn near a pub where I got kneed by a Scouser being friendly.

I slept on the grass here, in 20 minute snatches, wrapped in a copy of the European, because it was cold, after at least 5 bottles of wine. Carcassonne. 2nd December 1991.

*May the mountains of your pain
and experience
Be summits from which you see
the sunlit landscape of your life*

In A Most Dreary Garden

Walking dark alleyed with fear
Cobbles, black tarred in part
But all with the smell of decay

Talking in glassed gardens so drear
No wobbles in your strong heart
That's scarred with the knell
                          of the fray

Let's wag tongues
                from there to here
Deal the card in your mart
Fork a rose bed till breaking day
Hope it well well watered
                    with come what may

Fifteen

Sixteen

Sunset from my head
The Hole in the Wall Scarborough

Bomber

Standing on an iris brink
    On an edge of blue
        So clear and cold
May I fall with grace
      from God
Through the black
        to fields of gold
Landing with no time to think
In a light that's true
Let truth be tolled
May our tongues be laced
        And lies unshod
Through the flak
        Let our lives
            enfold

Some stories of the contents

Cover. . . . A combination of a Walburga and a poster for a Tong Theatre production of Joe Orton's 'A Good and Faithful Servant.' I was the servant.
Inside cover . . . Top poem-possibly the second Walburga. Second poem – see page 5.
Page (2) . . . . No idea which year this card was for, like many others. I have typeset the poem at least 4 different ways, so far.
(3) . . . . Top part: Christmas card, probably 1987. Bottom: Christmas 1982 or 83.
(4) . . . . On the Karelian farm, where my mother grew up, my grandfather hand sowed and reaped grain . 1996. Variously typeset.
(5) . . . . Goes with the poem on the inside cover. 1993.
(6-7) . . . . Christmas card. I have little clue as to the year.
(8) . . . . Picture and poem: Christmas card, probably very early 80's. Drawings: Northern Blast - incorporating Southern Wind. Issue No. 5, 1991.
(9) . . . . 4th August 1993 (ed).
(10) . . . . Written about a troubled place and time (ed).
(11) . . Both pictures were drawn on blank postcards, photocopied and then posted.
(12) . . . . Top: ? Bottom: 1990.
(13) . . . . The picture is a scan, of a photocopy, of a colour original.
(14) . . . . I have no clue as to the date, but very early (ed).
(15) Derry, Bradford City pre-season tour. 1993. I wrote the poem on page 32 nearby.
(16-17) . . . . Possibly originally drawn on a big beer mat.
(18) . . . . AKA Bomber. Based on love and a radio play. Feb. 1995.
(19) . . . . This page was the hardest to write, and took longest to set
(20-21) . . . . For some forgotten reason I did 2 different cards this year. The poem goes with the 'wavy' image. 1992.
(22) . . . . No idea why I wrote this on a french dictionary with chalk, at 1.30m of an October morn.
(23) . . . . Christmas 1993. (ed).
(24-25) . . . . Last hand drawn Walburga, to date. 1997.
(26 & 27) . . . . Birthday cards. One done for St. Crispin's Day, 25th October.
(28) . . . . Possibly the first Walburga. (?) 1987
(29 & 30) . . . . Both mid-Nineties.
(32) The opening's from my first experience of a Irish pub, on Piccadilly Circus, 1981. I Thought the barman had forgotten me, so I reached for my pint!
Inside Back. This was an A5 sheet, folded to A7. 3 of the pictures are made from the rose, or parts of the rose, drawn in the 4th. The colours are from time wrought changes to petals, stamens and sepal since (?) 1990.
Back Cover. In my picture, from a Bradford Playhouse/Priestley Centre production, I am playing Hwel, a dwarf, Welsh genius. I had to dig deep for for this. I took the picture of my mother in a Finnish folk museum.

(ed) means the original poem has been edited at some time.

Let calm be the sea
May your blessings flow free
Blessed balm for your troubles
And your radiance
　All come to see

Heart racing for flight
Vain pounding for fight
Hopes burning so fast
Melting memory to caste
May passion ignite
Belief be the light
Endure the ashes that are past
The love's what will last
Metaphor disguised in obscure
For your beauty must endure
My discounted heart
Loves, and my soul's torn apart.

REGINA

By the light of celestial
    fires

By the sound of the
    trump that cries

Above the playing of
    loveless lyres

You are beautiful
    within my eyes.

glyn watkins

written with chalk on a Collins French-English
English-French Dictionary at 1.30am 27th Oct 94

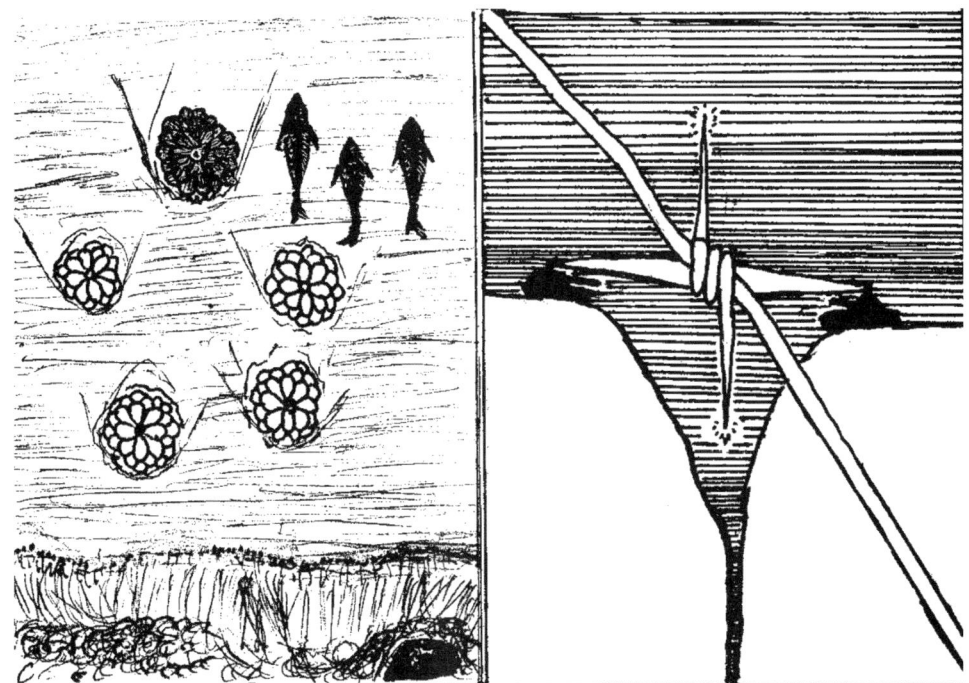

In the orchard
or on the wire

There's always blindness
that fear can sire

But tend the flame
that burns within

Find the stars
in the darkest mire
warm despair, and begin
to follow the path
to love's fire

Flowers on a flowing race
Dropped from the hearts
secret place
Floating with the flow of seasons
A mark of laughter
and of lesions
Their colour will not
change their ending
Like us they will flow on
past amending
May your stream be full and clear
and carry blooms of those
that hold you dear
May your waters be free of dam
or capture
And the scent of love
your heart enrapture

Hands that are tied
by fears unfaced
by excuses untraced
by desires ungraced

Power's always lied
it leads us to haste
it leads us grim paced
it leads all to waste

Hands held still
when life's cried
palms that are faced
whilst hope's pattern's
              are traced
Are by love's strong pull
              graced
Let your vision run wide
      unblinkered by pride
           with joy in your stride

This day is
called the feast
Crispian: He that
outlives this day,
and comes safe home,
will stand a tip-toe
when this day is named,
And rouse himself at the
name of Crispian.
He that shall live this day,
and see old age, will yearly
on the vigil feast his neighbours,
And say, 'Tomorrow is saint Crispian.'

On St Crispin's day

Bardic vaunting of Crispin's day
Cries deadly shaft
                not cherub's feather
T'was not love laid bleeding
                in the frey
On the feast of the saint of leather
But still life's warmed
                by sun shafted ray
Neither shame nor glory
                last forever
And to mark your living
                let me prey
That joy and your life
                be bound together

Myths and legends shown in glory
Faith and virtue are the story
But have we the power to understand
Tales that stand on shifting sand
The sword a symbol to those that pray
Can cut those down who do not pay
The dragons that lie beyond our ken
Can be painted by fears of poor weak men
Chivalric grail and armour bright
They will fail against time's chill knight
But those not drunk on power's strong wine
Can sip the chalice of love sublime
Your beauty will never fade or wilt
Against a radiance time can't tilt
May your soul be wrapped in arms of rapture
My vision of your grace
Time can never capture

Verdant fire of my soul
Joyous soundings go on further
On frost sharp mornings hear the toll
That thou be my bright Walburga

Duly a joy

Passing fancies
Passing time
Passing waves
of mis-spelt rhyme
And reasons
In seasons
Of love blinded mime
Coming together
Coming at all
The coming of winter
The knowledge of fall
The burning of leaving
The grip of thy thrall
The melting of meaning
To sweet nothing at all
Smoke it comes duly
A scented soft mist
Or flame lighted pall
My cheek is touch burning
To the heart of the yearning
For the spring of thy summer
And thy warmth burnished call

To The Eye of a Gale

Dark eyes drawing
In a market of flesh
Dark thoughts of meat
A weight, by cost
Stark lies pouring
When souls don't mesh
Joy so fleet
Await those lost
BUT
Mark life scoring
With desire that's fresh
Mark soul's heat
When rapture tossed
With beauty's soaring
Dark eye's
That still
      My warring.
      I'm lost!

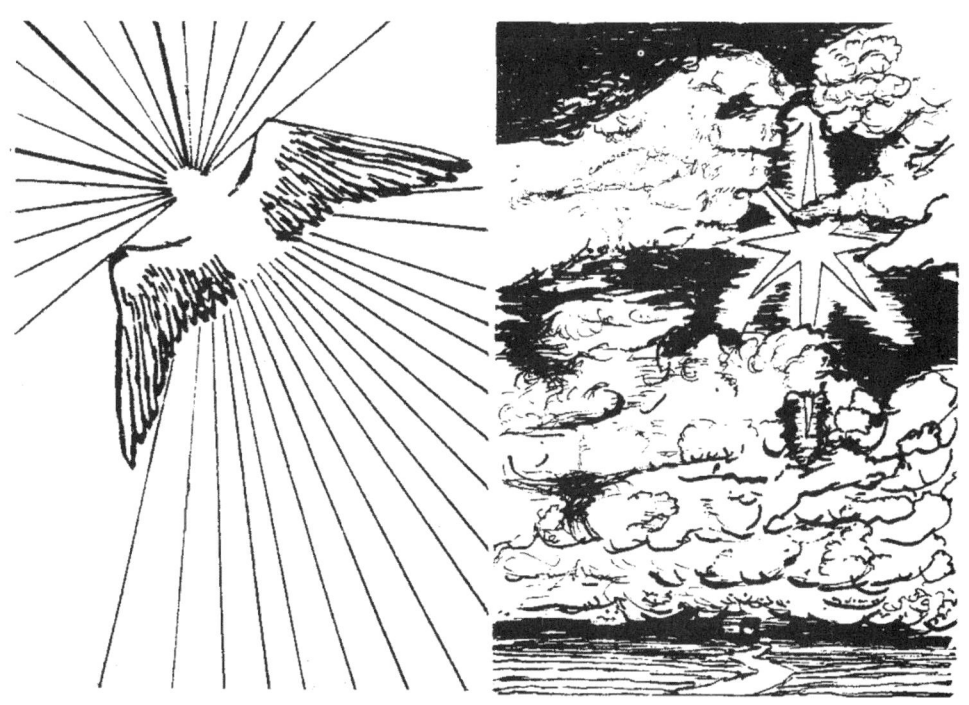

Repeating caper
Existing's chancy
Glowing star
Living soul

Darkness defeating
Glory resisting
Far flowing
Blessed with giving

Fist of vapour
Flight of fancy
Fire can mar
Sight of the goal

Fortune kissed
With shining light
Let hope be the sire
of a future bright

THE IRISH
THE STOUT

NOW YOU WAIT UNTIL IT'S BLACK AND WHITE TIME, AND THE LAWS OF NATURE WILL SEE YOU RIGHT. SETTLING WILL COME, AFTER A PAUSE. THE SETTLING OF HEADS, DEBTS AND LAWS. WITH BLURRING VISION, A BRAIN LIKE FISSION, BUT WILL WE ADMIT THE CAUSE? WE ALL KNOW THE TRUTH INDEED (IT'S ALWAYS STITCHED TO PREJUDICE OR CREED) WE ALWAYS BELIEVE IT WILL BREED (LIKE WARMTH IN THE MOUTHS OF HOARS)

Glyn Watkins
July 1993
Written in the Gweedor bar, Derry.